VOLTAIRE'S
Alphabet of Wit

EDITED AND ILLUSTRATED

BY PAUL McPHARLIN

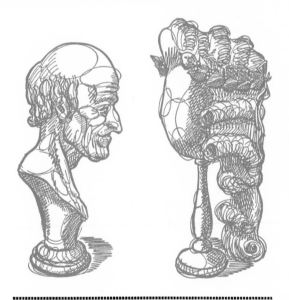

THE PETER PAUPER PRESS

MOUNT VERNON, NEW YORK

VOLTAIRE'S
ALPHABET OF WIT

■■■■■■■■■■■■■■■■■■■■■■■■■■■■■■■

The articles in this Alphabet of Wit *first appeared as* Questions on the Encyclopedia, *then were reprinted as* Reason by Alphabet, *both small pocket volumes. After Voltaire's death, however, these little rapier-thrusts were padded with many of his other papers into the eight-volume* Philosophical Dictionary. *In selecting them for a new pocket volume, we restore the author's original intention. It has been tempting to add a word here and there, by way of compensation for the many words deleted from the more prolix and untidy writings; but these added words, if not Voltaire's, are well within the vocabulary of his intention.*

ADAM

WHY WAS THERE such secrecy about Adam throughout the habitable earth, save in Palestine, until the time when Hebrew scriptures began to be known in Alexandria?

Such is the mystery of Providence, that the father and mother of the human race might have been totally unknown to their descendants — for the names of Adam and Eve are to be found in no ancient author of Greece, Rome, Persia, or Syria, nor even of the Arabs until the time of Mahomet — had it not been God's pleasure that the origin of the great family of the world be concealed from all but the smallest and most unfortunate part of that family.

Nothing will here be said of Adam's second wife, Lilith, given him by the ancient rabbis.

5

Very little family gossip has come down to us. Indeed, the pious Mme. de Bourignon was sure that Adam was a hermaphrodite, like the first men of the divine Plato. God had revealed a very intimate secret to her; but as I have not had the same revelation, I say nothing of the matter.

ADULTERY

THIS term is not heard in good company. We do not say, "Madame la Duchesse lives in adultery with Monsieur le Chevalier," or "Madame la Marquise has criminal relations with Monsieur l'Abbé." We say, "This week Monsieur l'Abbé is the lover of Madame la Marquise." Ladies discussing with their friends their adulteries remark, "I confess I'm rather fond of him." They used to confess they felt "some esteem," but since the time a certain wife told her confessor that she had esteem for a high official, and he asked how many proofs of esteem there had been given, ladies of quality have esteemed no one — and gone but little to confession.

About the year 1764 a French judge was so unfortunate as to marry a woman who had been led astray by a priest, and who continued to waver of her own accord. He was obliged to leave her. Being, however, but forty and in lusty health, he needed a companion. Too scrupulous to seek another man's wife, and too fearful to consort with prostitutes, he pleaded earnestly with the Church:

"My wife erred and I am the one to suffer. A woman is necessary to me. Without one how can I keep my virtue? Yet you refuse her to me; I cannot marry another. You compel me to take pleasure which you reprobate or consolation which you condemn. You force me to be a criminal. Your priests and monks may abstain from women if need be; I have no objections. It checks the increase in population. They suffer misfortune they have contrived for themselves. But I, a judge who serves mankind all day, have need of a little womankind at night."

Then there was the Countess D'Arcira of Portugal, a wife who made this plea before a junta: "The Gospels forbid adultery both to my husband and me. He has been guilty of fifty infidelities—he gave my necklace to one woman, my earrings to another — and I have imitated him only once, and then with the handsomest young man in Lisbon. Must I then answer questions before a panel of men, any one of whom would lose no time in such nonsense if he were alone with me? Must I have this lovely hair cut off? Must I be confined with nuns? Must I be deprived of the fortune I brought my husband so that he can go on with his seductions and adulteries? Is this justice?"

It would appear that, in order to assure a just verdict in an action for adultery, the jury should be composed of six men and six women, and — in the event of a tie — a hermaphrodite to cast the deciding vote.

ANIMALS

WHAT a pitiful and sorry thing to say that animals are mere mechanisms, bereft of understanding and feeling! What of the bird that builds its nest in a semicircle when attaching it to a wall, in a quarter circle when in a corner, and in a complete circle on a branch? What of the hunting dog that you train for three months; doesn't he know more than when you started?

Is it because I can speak to you that you judge me to have feeling, memory, and ideas? If I did not speak, and you saw me come in looking downcast, searching anxiously for a paper, opening the desk where I remember having shut it, then finding it and joyfully reading it, would you not judge that I felt distress and pleasure, that I had memory and understanding? Apply the same judgment to a dog that has lost its master, that goes searching for him up and down every road, whimpering, that comes in and goes up and down stairs and from room to room, until it finds him at last in his study, and giving yelps of delight, jumps and caresses him.

Scholastics ask whether animals have a soul. I do not understand their question. A tree can pull the sap into its fibers and unfold the buds of its leaves and blossoms; does it have a soul? It has received certain faculties. Animals have those of feeling, memory, and ideas. Who has given them these faculties? Who has made the grass of the fields to grow, and the earth to revolve about the sun?

APPEARANCES

ARE all appearances deceptive? Have our senses been given us only to trick us? Is everything error? Do we live in a dream? We see the sun still setting when it is below the horizon. A square tower seems to be round. A straight stick in water seems to be bent. You see your face in a mirror; the image appears to be behind the glass when it is neither behind nor before it. The glass itself, seemingly so smooth and even, is made up of tiny projections and pits. The fairest skin is a bristling net of minute hairs. What is large to us is small to an elephant; what is small may be a whole world to an insect.

Nothing is either as it appears to be, or where we think it is. Philosophers, weary of being deceived, have in their petulance declared that nothing exists but what is in our mind. They might have gone all the way and concluded that, mind being as elusive as matter, there is nothing real either in matter or mind. Perhaps it is in this despair of ever knowing anything that certain Chinese philosophers say that Nothing is the beginning and end of all things.

You do not see the net of hairs of the white and delicate skin you idolize. Organisms a thousand times less than a mite perceive what escapes your vision; they lodge, feed, and travel about on it as in an extensive country; those on a right arm are ignorant that creatures of their own species exist on a left. If you were so unfortunate as to see what they see, this charming skin would transfix you with horror.

All is in due proportion. The laws of optics, which show you an object where it is not, make the sun appear two feet in diameter when it is a million times larger than the earth, a size impossible for your eye to encompass. Our senses assist much more than they deceive us.

Motion, time, hardness, softness, size, distance, appearances, all are relative. And who has created the delicate adjustment of relativities?

BEAUTY

TO A TOAD what is beauty? A female with two lovely pop-eyes, a wide mouth, yellow belly, and green spotted back. To a Negro of Guinea what is beauty? A black oily skin, blubber lips, a flat nose. To the devil? Horns, claws, and a tail. To the philosophers? Ask them and they reply in jargon. One night I sat next to a philosopher at a play. "How beautiful it is!" he exclaimed. "In what way?" I inquired. "It has," he replied, "achieved its end."

The next day I met the same philosopher after he had taken some effective medicine. "It has achieved its end," I remarked. "It must be very beautiful." After some discussion he concluded that beauty is relative, just as what may be de-

10

cent in Japan is indecent in Rome, or what may be fashionable in Paris is not so in Peking. That saved him the trouble of composing a long dissertation on beauty.

BOOKS

So you think nothing of books, you who strive for great things, or pleasure, or prefer indolence? Remember that the whole world, save only the savage parts, is under the sway of books. Northern Africa and western Asia obey the Koran. China is ruled by the books of Confucius, and much of India by the Vedas. Persia was governed for ages by the books of one of the Zoroasters.

If you get into a lawsuit or criminal trial, your property, your honor, and perhaps your life depend on the interpretation of books you have never read. There are mediocre books to be sure; but among both books and men a small number play a large part.

Perhaps it will hardly be believed that Dr. Tamponet maintained, "I could set out to find a number of heresies in the Lord's Prayer (which we know to have come from Divine lips) if it had just been published by a Jesuit. Thus: 'Our Father, which art in heaven,' — a proposition tending toward heresy, because God is everywhere. — 'Thy kingdom come, Thy will be done on earth as it is in heaven' — more heresy, for again and again Scriptures say that God already reigns eternally and universally; moreover, it is rash to ask that His will be done, since nothing is or can be done but by the will of God. — 'Give us this day our daily bread' — a proposition directly contrary to Jesus' 'Take no thought, saying what shall we eat, or what shall we drink.' — 'Forgive us our debts as we forgive our debtors' — a rash proposition which compares man to God, destroys gratuitous predestination, and assumes that God is bound to do to us as we do to others; besides, no convent in Europe ever remitted to its farmers a single penny. — 'Lead us not into temptation,' — a proposition scandalous and manifestly heretical, for there is no tempter but the devil. You see, then," said Dr. Tamponet, "that there is nothing, be it ever so venerable, but that may be given a twist for the worse."

If you publish a book, a parish curate accuses you of heresy, a college sophomore denounces you, an illiterate condemns you, the public derides you, your publisher renounces you, and your wine dealer cuts off your credit. I always add to my prayers, "Deliver me, O Lord, from the itch of bookmaking."

CANNIBALS

In 1725 four savages were brought from the Mississippi to Fontainebleau. I had the honor of conversing with them. Among them was a young woman whom I asked if she had eaten men. "Of course," she answered with great simplicity. I appeared to be a little scandalized, whereupon she continued, "Is it not better to eat one's dead enemy than to leave him to be devoured by wild beasts? And surely victors deserve the spoils." We kill our neighbors in fights or skirmishes, and for the most trifling reasons, then leave them to the crows and worms. In killing is the horror and the crime; what does it matter when a man is dead whether he be eaten by a soldier or by a vulture?

CELIBACY

THE first Christians did not consider celibacy a virtue. Nearly all the apostles and disciples were married. St. Paul wrote to Titus, "Choose for a priest him who is the husband of one wife, having believing children, and not under accusation of dissoluteness." The proceedings of the Council of Nice on the subject of married priests deserve attention. Some bishops proposed that priests thenceforward put away their wives, but St. Paphnucius the Martyr strenuously opposed it, observing that marriage was chastity; and

statue where the strapping lads are shown frightened out of several years' growth. All this happened, naturally, when cities that had been built by the gods were taken by armies hidden in a wooden horse, when rivers on occasion flowed backwards, water was changed to blood, and both the sun and moon had a way of standing still upon the slightest provocation.

There was surely enchantment in those days!

Enchantments to kindle love were hawked by the Jews in ancient Rome and Alexandria, and are still sold in parts of Asia. You can read in Apuleius how he was accused by a Christian whose daughter he had married of having bewitched her by philters. It was claimed that these were made of fish, and Venus having been born of the sea, fish were supposed to have a great amorous influence. Apuleius was accused of having used, specifically, periwinkles, lobster patties, female sea-urchins, spiced oysters, and squid, celebrated for its fertility.

What he really used to enchant the Christian's daughter was neither music nor love-potion, as he explained. He admitted the girl had called him a magician. "But," said he, "if she had called me a consul that wouldn't make me one."

When some of our debilitated rakes took chocolate because of a reputation it enjoyed among them, they could take twenty cups without becoming any more winning. Youth and health are the greatest philters.

ENGLISH DRAMA

I HAVE been looking through a new edition of Shakespeare made by one Samuel Johnson. He remarks that foreigners are obtuse when they are surprised to find a comic Roman senator or a drunken king on the stage in the plays of the great Shakespeare. I do not wish to hint that this Mr. Johnson is a sorry jester or too fond of his drink, but I do find it rather extraordinary that he includes slapstick and inebriety among the beauties of tragedy. His reasons are no less curious. He says that the dramatist disdains accidental embellishments — like the painter who, having got a figure done, pays little further attention to its drapery. The comparison would have been better had he spoken of a painter of heroic figures who introduced ridiculous grotesques among them.

The most singular point is that Shakespeare is really a genius. The Italian, French, and other men of letters who have not spent some time in his country take him only for a clown, a comic inferior to Harlequin, the most contemptible jack-a-pudding that ever played to the gallery. Yet it is this man who can exalt the imagination and stir the heart to its depths. It is Truth, it is Nature herself, speaking out in her own language without artificiality. This sublimity seems not of the author's seeking.

FICTION

Supposing that it brings home truth, what is wrong with fiction? Don't you like the story of the sultan who, disbelieving that a moment could be long, disputed with his dervish on the nature of duration? The latter, to convince him, asked him to put his head into a basin for a moment. Straightway the sultan found himself in a terrible desert; he had to live by the sweat of his brow; he married and had children who grew up to torment him; after five and twenty years he found his way back to his own country and palace, lifted his head, and saw the basin and dervish before him.

As for fiction which shows nothing and gets nowhere, what is it but untruth? Or fiction which rambles on from one unrelated situation to another, is it any better than a dream?

It may be pointed out that certain classic tales are incoherent, without ingenuity, and even absurd. If they are still admired it is because of their fine details rather than their general framework. I won't belabor the point, but if you seek bad reviews and to be condemned to oblivion, take one of those tales for your model.

GOVERNMENT

THERE must be some exquisite pleasure in governing, to judge from the numbers who are eager to be concerned in it. We have more books on government than governors in the world. I don't want to set myself up as an instructor to kings and their ministers, valets, confessors, and treasurers; I understand nothing about government. But it seems strange that with all our volumes on the subject, from Plato to Machiavelli, we are not all well acquainted with the duties of the heads of state.

Few nations are governed by themselves. It is not the English who reign in England: the king is of a German family which succeeded a Dutch prince who followed a Scotch family which had come from an Angevin family that had replaced a Norman family that had expelled a family of usurping Saxons. Rome had many emperors who were born in the barbarous provinces, and many popes born in provinces no less barbarous. Let him govern who can!

In 1769 a traveler reported on one of the countries he had seen in a world tour: "It had become involved with its neighbors in a war which was dubbed the Ridiculous because much was lost and nothing was gained by it. At the conclusion of peace, it was in the most dreadful state of misery; it had lost money, soldiers, fleet, and commerce. It seemed a nation absolutely annihilated, and this was a pity, for a great part of the people were amiable, industrious, and gay. Yet at the end of two years its capital and principal cities were more opulent than ever. Luxury had increased, and an air of enjoyment prevailed everywhere. It was only after I had examined the governments of the neighboring nations that I could discover the cause of what appeared so unaccountable. I found that those governments were just as bad as those of this nation, but that this nation was superior to all the rest in industry."

HAPPINESS

CAN one man be happier than another? It is clear that a man who has the gout and stone, who has lost his money, his good name, his wife and family, and who is about to be hanged after having been mangled, is less happy than a young, vigorous sultan, or La Fontaine's cobbler. But how are we to determine which is the happier of two men equally healthy, prosperous, and placed in society? Their temperaments must decide it. The most moderate, the least worrisome, the most keenly perceptive is the most happy; but unfortunately the most keenly perceptive is often the least moderate. It is not our position, but our disposition, which renders us happy. Our disposition depends upon the functioning of our organs, over which we have no control.

HELL

THE poets, having invented the infernal regions, were the first to laugh at them. In the *Aeneid* Virgil sometimes mentions hell seriously because that suits his subject, and sometimes he speaks of it with contempt. Marcus Aurelius philosophically reasons, "He who fears death fears either to be deprived of all senses, or to experience new sensations. If one no longer retains his own senses he will no longer be subject to pain or grief for, being totally different, he will have senses of a different nature."

When men came to a social organization they must have perceived that a great number of criminals eluded the severity of the laws; it was necessary to establish a check; this was to be found only in religion. The Persians, Chaldaeans, Egyptians, and Greeks thus created the idea of punishments after the present life; and of all the nations of antiquity that we are acquainted with, only the Jews admitted punishment on earth alone. But among them the Pharisees and Essenians did admit, according to certain notions of their own, a belief in hell. This dogma had passed from the Greeks to the Romans and was adopted by the Christians. Yet many of the fathers of the Church rejected the doctrine of eternal punishment. It appeared to them absurd that an unfortunate man should burn throughout eternity for stealing a goat. When the time comes in which no one any longer believes in hell, what restraint will there be upon wickedness? Why, there will be a feeling of honor, and the restraint of the laws — and that of the Deity Himself whose will it is that mankind be just, whether there be a hell or not.

HISTORY

HISTORY is the recital of facts represented as true. Fable, on the other hand, is the recital of facts represented as fiction. As for the history of man's ideas, unfortunately this is nothing more than the chronicle of human error.

Periods are distinguished as either fabulous or historical. But even in historic times it is necessary to separate truth from fable. Was it very likely that Romulus, the grandson of the king of the Sabines, was compelled to carry off the Sabine women in order to get wives for his men? Is the history of the chaste Lucretia highly probable? Does the adventure of Regulus, in the hogshead stuck round with iron spikes, deserve belief? Would not Polybius, a contemporary, have recorded it had it been true?

We might naturally be led to think that a monument erected to commemorate an event would attest its certainty. Then does the famous statue of Laocoon furnish incontestable evidence of the truth of the story of the Trojan horse? One of our own most ancient monuments is a figure of St. Denis shown carrying his head in his hands. Portraits frequently show more of an inclination toward display than toward the historic record.

Certainty not based upon mathematical demonstration is only probability; most history must be that. When Marco Polo described the greatness and the people of China, being the first and for a time the only western writer who had described them, he was not believed. The Portuguese, who later came into communication with that vast empire through trade with it, began to make the description probable. It is now a matter of certainty, for thousands of witnesses from different nations know about it, unopposed by contrary testimony.

History is sometimes shamefully abused, even in England. As there are always two parties there in a state of pitched battle, until some common cause unites them for a season, the writings of one faction condemn everything that the other approves. The same individual is represented as a Cato and a Cataline. Perhaps the truth may be discovered only in whatever good the party historian allows his opponents, and whatever bad he imputes to his own chiefs.

IGNORANCE

SOME there are who are so ashamed of all they do not know that they strive to disguise themselves either as wits or philosophers.

Why do we live? Why is there life? What is awareness? How do I happen to have it? How can my ear translate the vibration of air into the sensation of sound, or my eye the freighting of light into color? Of the basic mystery of all this I am profoundly ignorant, and shall always be.

What is thought? Where does it lodge? How does it happen? How do my thoughts take shape while I dream? Do I think because I will to do so? No, for as I dream, and often while I am awake, my ideas run counter to what I would have them. Ideas long forgotten and put away in the attic of my memory suddenly come to light without any effort or volition, often when I had long searched in vain for them.

Why has man, of all the species of animals, alone the mad ambition to dominate his fellows? Why do so many invite death in the attempt to satisfy this ambition?

Why do the vast numbers in India, deceived and enslaved by their bonzes, in subjugation to the descendant of a Tartar, bowed down by labor, groaning in misery, assailed by disease, and a mark for all the scourges of famine and plague, still cling fondly to life? Whence comes evil; why does it exist?

O my fellow atoms of a day! O my comrades in littleness, born like me to suffer everything and be ignorant of everything! Are there really among you any so completely deluded that you imagine you know the answers to all these questions? No; in the bottom of your hearts you can feel your own nothingness as completely as I. But still you are arrogant and conceited enough to wish us to embrace your vain systems. Not having the power to tyrannize over our bodies, you aspire to become the tyrants of our spirit!

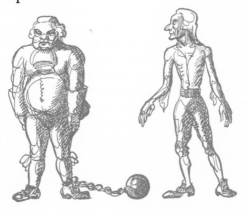

IMPOTENCE

THE canon law made considerable to-do of the question of impotence. Might a man who was prevented by sorcery from consummating his first marriage, after being divorced and having children by a second wife — might he, on the death of the second, still reject his first wife should she lay claim to him? All the great canonists decided in the negative: De Nevo, Alberic, Turrecremata, Soto, and fifty more.

It is impossible to help admiring the sagacity exhibited by the canonists, especially for the knowledge those irreproachable celibates had of the mysteries of sexual intercourse. There is no aberration, however strange, on which they did not hold forth. They discussed at length all the cases in which capability may exist at one time, and impotence in another. They inquired into all the ingenious devices to assist nature, and with the avowed object of pronouncing what is allowable and what is not, exposed all which might have remained veiled.

Sanchez especially distinguished himself by collecting cases of conscience which the boldest wife would hesitate to submit to her most prudent confidante. One query led to another in interminable succession, until the ultimate was reached in the extraordinary examination of the manner of communication of the Holy Ghost with the Virgin Mary.

Such exhaustive researches had never before been made, and could never have been made save by theologians.

Marriage having arrived in the course of time at the dignity of a sacrament, the ecclesiastics naturally became judges of all which took place between husband and wife, and not only that, but also all which did *not* take place.

Wives possessed the right to present a request to be *embesognées* — the French term, though the proceedings were carried on in Latin. Clerks pleaded and priests pronounced judgment, to determine these points: whether a man was bewitched — or a woman merely wanted another husband.

The most important proof of capability required from persons accused of impotence was that called "the congress." This combat in an enclosed field was adopted in France in the fourteenth century. It was not conducted exactly as people have imagined. It was supposed that a conjugal consummation took place under the inspection of physicians, surgeons, and midwives, but such was not the case. The parties went to bed in the usual manner, and at a proper time the inspectors, waiting in the next room, were called in to pronounce upon the case.

In the famous process of the Marquis de Langeais, decided in 1659, milord demanded the congress; but thanks to the management of his lady, Marie de St. Simon, did not succeed. He demanded a second trial but the judges, tired of the outcries of the superstitious, the plaints of the prudes, and the raillery of the wits, refused it. They declared the marquis impotent and his marriage void, forbade him to marry again, and allowed his wife to take another husband.

But the Marquis disregarded this sentence, married the lovely Diana de Navailles, and by her had seven children!

INCUBI

HAVE there ever been incubi and succubi? Even though you doubt it, our learned jurisconsults and demonologists have proved both to exist.

It is supposed that Satan, always a very busy person, spends time producing heated dreams in young ladies and gentlemen, and by a sort of double process achieves the same end which resulted in so many heroes and demigods of old. He certainly took superfluous trouble, for he could have left the young people alone, and without his assistance the world would have been sufficiently supplied with heroes.

The ancient gods frequently disguised themselves, in the pursuit of human girls, as eagles, pigeons, swans, horses, or showers of gold, but the goddesses assumed no disguise, having only to show themselves to gain their objective. It is presumed that, whatever shapes the gods took, they consummated their loves in the convenient and more compatible form of men.

In accepting a demonistic scheme (less noble

and decorous than that of the deities of antiquity) we believed a girl might be rendered pregnant by the ministry of the devil. We cannot doubt that this is possible, for the Sorbonne decided it to be true in 1318, and the decision has never been revoked. We are bound to believe in incubi and succubi, because our professors have evidently always believed in them. And not only they. Bodin, in his book about sorcerers, tells of Jean Hervilier, a native of Verberie, who was condemned by the Parliament of Paris to be burned alive for having prostituted his daughter to the devil. We learn that the embraces of this personage, who appeared as a big

of Judith before she cut off the head of Holofernes in bed; it is not actually mentioned, but is probable enough. In *Othello* the Moor gives his wife two kisses before smothering her. To some, this seems quite dreadful, but others cite it as a fine touch of realism, especially for a Moor.

Kissing has long been the approved manner of greeting ladies in France, Italy, Germany, and England. But there is a grave danger to be noted. A system of nerves connects the lips to the heart and lower regions; a kiss is therefore an especially dangerous sensation. Virtue may well suffer from a prolonged and ardent kiss between two young pietists of eighteen.

The early Christians of both sexes kissed at their *agapae* or love feasts. They bestowed the holy kiss, the kiss of peace, and the brotherly and sisterly kiss. Though it lasted four centuries, this custom was finally abolished in distrust of the consequences. It drew on the Christians, when they were little known, imputations of debauchery from the priests of Jupiter and the priestesses of Vesta. We read in Petronius and other authors that dissolute Romans called one another brother and sister, and it was assumed that the Christians did so with no better intent. Innocently they gave occasion for scandal.

It is remarkable that only mankind and turtledoves practice kissing — from the latter comes the Latin word *columbatim*, which cannot very well be rendered in our language. We cannot properly dwell longer on this interesting subject, although Montaigne remarks, "It should be discussed without reserve; we speak right out of killing, wounding, betraying, while of this we whisper."

LOVE

THERE are so many kinds of love that, in defining it, one must be specific. Some apply the term to a caprice of a few days, a connection without attachment, a passion without affection, a pretense, a gallantry, a mere ceremony, a romantic fancy, a taste followed quickly by distaste. It is applied to innumerable fantasies.

Should a philosopher be inclined to make an exhaustive research into so unlikely a subject, he might well begin with Plato's *Symposium*, wherein Socrates, the decent and honorable lover of Alcibiades and Agathon, converses with them on love's metaphysics. Lucretius speaks of it as a philosopher; so does Virgil.

It is an imaginative embroidery on the stuff of nature. Look at the sparrows in your garden; see your doves; observe the bull as he meets the heifer; regard that powerful, spirited stallion which a couple of your grooms are leading to the mare who quietly waits, evidently pleased at his approach; catch the flash in his eye, hear his resonant, melodious neighing, pay heed to his springing and curveting, his pointed ears, his mouth open and convulsively gasping, his distended nostrils, his fiery breath, his erect, waving mane, and the impetuosity with which he rushes toward what nature has destined for him; do not, however, envy him his pleasure, but reflect on the advantages which the human species have in love, as a compensation for the strength, beauty and celerity of mere animals.

Most of the animals which copulate take pleasure through but a single sense; when appetite is satisfied, all is over. No animal but man knows fondling; his whole body is sensitive to it; his lips particularly experience an unwearying delight which belongs to his species alone; finally, he is alive to the endearments of love at all seasons, while mere animals know them only for limited periods. If you reflect on this lofty preëminence, you will agree with the Earl of Rochester's remark that love would impel a whole nation of atheists to worship God.

As men have a faculty of perfecting what nature has bestowed, they have improved upon the gift of love. Cleanliness, good care, and health render the body more sensitive and increase its capacity for pleasure. All amiable and estimable qualities merge into love, as metals amalgamate with gold; friendship and respect rally to its support; excellence both of mind and body strengthens its bonds.

Such are the advantages possessed by man over the animals. But if he has pleasures unknown to them, how many pains does he have that they are free of! The most dreadful of these come from a disease to which man alone is subject, which has poisoned the pleasures of love and sources of life over most of the globe. This is not, like other maladies, a consequence of excess. It was not introduced through debauchery. The Phrynes and Laïses, the Floras and Messalinas, never had it. It originated in islands where man dwelt in innocence, whence it has spread throughout the civilized world. If nature could be accused of despising her own work, thwarting her own scheme, and quarreling with her own impulses it would be in this horrible scourge. And can this then be, in the best of all possible worlds? If Caesar and Anthony and Octavius never had the disease, why should Francis I have died of it? Things seem to be so ordered — unfortunately for those to whom Rabelais dedicated his book.

MARRIAGE

St. Augustine approved marriages of the orthodox with heretics, for he hoped that the faithful spouse would convert the other; and Louis XIV condemned them, lest the heterodox should pervert the believer.

Once I met a motto merchant who recited to me some of his best stock items: "Induce citizens to marry as early as possible. Let them be tax-exempt the first year, passing on their assessments to those of the same age who remain unmarried.

"The more married men there are, the fewer

will be the crimes. Look at the criminal court news: you'll see a hundred youths indicted to one father of a family.

"Marriage makes a man wiser and more virtuous. The father of a family hesitates to make a fool of himself before his children, or to give them shame for their inheritance.

"Let soldiers marry; they will no longer desert. Bound to their families, they are bound to their country. An unmarried soldier is often nothing but a vagabond, caring little whether he serves the King of Naples or of Morocco."

Roman soldiers were married. They fought for their wives and children and made slaves of the wives and children of other nations.

A great Italian politician said to me when I was young, "*Caro figlio*, remember that the Jews had one pretty good practice: they abhorred virginity. If that superstitious little nation of jobbers hadn't regarded marriage as the first of human obligations, if they had set up convents of nuns, they would surely have been goners."

MORALITY

I HAVE just read in a fourteen-volume history, "The Christians had a morality, but the pagans had none." What nonsense; what of the morality of Socrates, of Zaleucus, of Charondas, of Cicero, of Epictetus and Marcus Aurelius?

There is but one morality, as there is but one geometry. You say that most men know little about geometry. True; but if they study it ever so little, they all draw the same conclusions. Farmers, factory hands, laborers, do not take courses in morality; they read neither Cicero's *De Finibus* nor Aristotle's *Ethics*, yet the moment they start to think they are disciples of Cicero. The Indian dyer, the Tartar shepherd, and the English sailor know justice and injustice. Confucius did not invent a system of morals; he found it in the hearts of mankind.

There is no morality in superstition. There is none in ceremonial. It has nothing to do with dogma. Dogmas differ, but morality is the same among all men who make use of their reason. Morality proceeds from God, like light; superstition is only darkness.

MOUNTAIN

THE fable of the mountain which after terrifying the whole countryside with its screams of labor pain, brought forth, to the ridicule of all, a mouse, is an ancient one and a universal. But those who ridiculed it were not philosophers. Rather than mocking they should have admired. A mountain being delivered of a mouse is quite as extraordinary, quite as worthy of admiration, as a mouse being delivered of a mountain. A rock producing a rat — even that would have been prodigious; the world has never seen anything to approach it. All the constellations in the universe could not bring forth a fly. And so, where the stupid mock, the philosopher marvels; where the insensitive stare in astonishment, he often smiles.

NOVELTY

THE first words of Ovid's *Metamorphoses*, "In nova fert animus," might be taken as the motto of mankind. Nobody gets very much excited by the wonderful spectacle of sunrise, which can be seen every day, but a lot of people run to gape at the smallest meteor that plummets through the autumn sky. We despise what is common or what has long been known. Book shops will not burden themselves with Virgil or Horace, only with the new best sellers, no matter how bad. And the clerks take you aside and say, "We've just got in a shipment from abroad."

Women have ever complained that men desert them for what has no merit but its novelty. And ladies — I regret to say, for I have infinite respect for them — give men the same cause to complain.

Perhaps this widespread hunger for novelty is a benefit of nature. We are told, "Be content with what you have. Desire no more than you deserve. Quell your restless spirits." These are good maxims. But if we had followed them we should still be feeding on acorns and sleeping under the stars, and should have had no Corneille, Racine, Molière — or Voltaire.

OPTIMISM

According to Plato, Divinity chose the best of all possible worlds. This tenet has been accepted by many Christian philosophers, although it seems at cross-purposes with the doctrine of original sin. After the fall, this was no longer the best of all possible worlds. If it was ever so it might still be so; but many think it the worst of worlds instead of the best.

Leibnitz takes the part of Plato. Since readers complain that one is no clearer than the other, and I who have read them both more than once must agree with them; and since the gospel reveals nothing on the subject, I do not feel too badly at having to remain in the dark.

To be driven out of a delightful garden where we might have lived forever if only an apple hadn't been eaten — to bring forth poor children into misery, only that they may bring forth more — to be sick with so many diseases, vexed with so many disappointments, to die amidst grief, and in recompense to burn throughout eternity — is this the best of all possible lots? It certainly isn't good, so far as *we* are concerned; then how can it be so to God?

I dislike quoting; passages are too often cited out of context, and misconceptions ensue. But I must quote the early Christian father Lactantius, who, writing on the anger of God, causes Epicurus to say: "If God is willing to take evil from the world and cannot, He is not omnipotent. If He can but will not, He is not benevolent. If He is neither able nor willing, He is neither omnipotent nor benevolent. If He *is* both able and willing, how can evil exist?"

The origin of evil has always been a knotty problem. Thus many ancient philosophers resorted to a belief in two equal powers of good and evil. Not the least of absurdities is the presumption that two all-powerful beings, locked in the struggle for the world, should make a treaty like the two quacks in Molière: "Give me the clyster and I'll let you have the lancet."

Basilides maintained, with the Neoplatonists of the first century of the Church, that God gave the making of the world to some of His inferior angels who, being inexpert, produced what we have. This theological fable is brushed aside by the objection that it is not in the nature of a Deity all-powerful and all-wise to entrust the construction of a world to subcontractors, incompetent at that. Simon, sensing this objection, obviates it by saying that the slovenly angel was sent to damnation for his work; but roasting an angel makes no amends.

The Syrians had a pretty story about man and woman, who were created in the fourth heaven; they tried eating a cake, though ambrosia was their usual food; ambrosia was exhaled through the pores, but the cake made a new problem. They asked an angel to direct them to the W. C. "See that little globe down there?" he said. "That's the earth, the latrine of the universe."

Man and woman hastened down, and have been here, with evil, ever since.

Bolingbroke, Shaftesbury, and Pope, their industrious amanuensis, resolve the question of evil no better than the rest. Their "all for the best" says no more than that immutable laws govern everything. We learn very little when we remark, after the manner of little children, that flies are created to be eaten by spiders, spiders by swallows, swallows by hawks, hawks by eagles, eagles by men, and men by one another, to be food for worms, and finally (at least one out of a thousand) prey for devils.

There is a regular, recurring order of things for animals of all kinds. When a stone forms in my bladder, the mechanical process is wonderful: sandy particles come together, by the Newtonian laws of attraction, and form a stone which gradually increases, according to the regular order of things, and gives me the most exquisite sensation of pain. A surgeon, cunning in the art of Tubal Cain, cuts into me with a sharp instrument, severs the perineum, seizes the stone with his forceps (it breaks, during his labor, in the regular mechanical order of things), and in the same order of things I die in frightful torments. All this is "for the best," being in the obvious physical order of things; and I know as well as you do that I perish.

This system represents the Author of Nature as a powerful and malevolent monarch, who cares not a whit for the destruction of thousands of men, or for those who live in penury and tears, so long as He carries out His designs.

Philosophers who embrace the doctrine that this is the best of all possible worlds are therefore far from a comfortable solution. The question of good and evil remains in obscurest chaos for those who seek to fathom it. Let us place at the end of every chapter of metaphysics the two letters used by Roman judges when they did not understand a plea: N. L., *non liquet*, not clear.

PASSION

TELL me, doctor — I don't mean a doctor of medicine, who really has some degree of information, having dissected assiduously the human matrix to find something of how the thinking being is made; I mean a very different sort of person, a doctor of theology — tell me why it is that, your pretty young housekeeper having used a few endearing words and coquettish airs, your blood warms up, your whole body tingles with desire, and you partake of pleasures whereby is introduced into the world another being all sodden with original sin?

Please explain how the original action is connected with the result.

The next morning while you take your chocolate your memory recalls the pleasures of the night, and the scene comes back with all its rapture. Have you any idea, my fine automaton, what this process of memory, possessed by you in common with all animals, really is?

I perceive, doctor, by the words you have been stammering out, that you do not know what the soul is, and that you have been talking all your life without a clear idea of it. If you don't know, why not acknowledge it like an honest man?

In his irritation the doctor becomes agitated; blood rushes to his face; if he had been stronger than I, and had not been restrained by a sense of decency, he would certainly have struck me. His heart swells; the systole and diastole fail in their regular operation; his brain is congested and he falls down in a fit of apoplexy. What connection can there be between the blood, heart, and brain, and an opinion contrary to your own? I utter certain sounds — he utters certain sounds — and he drops dead!

Poor puppets of the Eternal Artificer, who know neither why nor how the invisible hand pulls the strings, at length to pack us away in our wooden box! We can only repeat with Aristotle, "All is hidden, all is secret."

QUACK

PHYSICIANS cling to cities; there are few of them in country places. Cities contain rich citizens; their maladies spring from debauchery, gluttony, and excitements.

The famous physician Dumoulin said when

dying, "I leave two great physicians behind me, simple food and pure water."

In 1728 a quack confided to some friends that his uncle, who had lived to the age of almost a hundred, and then had been killed by an accident, had left him the secret of a kind of water which would prolong life to one hundred and fifty, providing one lived sanely. When a funeral passed he would shrug and say, "Poor fellow, if he had only drunk my water!"

His friends who drank his water and followed his regimen found themselves in good health and praised its virtues. The quack then put it up in six-franc bottles and it sold prodigiously. It was nothing but Seine water with a pinch of salt in it, but those who made an effort at living sanely while they took it, and had good constitutions to begin with, soon found themselves cured of their indispositions.

Those who were not cured were told, "It's your own fault. Have you been temperate? Have you been continent? You see!"

When it was found out that it was only Seine water, people naturally took no more of it and resorted to other quacks. But he must be credited with doing no little good — he advised men to temperance. He just charged too much for the water.

Mahomet was upon the point of failure when the Arabs of Medina were persuaded that he was an intimate friend of the archangel Gabriel. Today if anybody in Constantinople should suggest that he was on amicable terms with Raphael, an archangel of even higher rank, he would risk public impaling.

Quacks should know their time.

QUERIES

WHY was not a tenth of the money lost in the war of 1741 used in helping and improving the country? If half the men killed to no purpose in Germany had lived, might not the state have been more flourishing? Why prefer a war to the happy labors of peace?

Why have nations reduced to extremity and humiliation still supported themselves in spite of all efforts to crush them? Is it not because they were active and industrious? Are not their people like bees: you take their honey and they work to produce more?

Why in pagan antiquity were there no theological disputes, or hostile sects?

Why do booksellers publicly display the *Course of Atheism* by Lucretius, why is it to be found, in handsome morocco, in the libraries of princes and bishops, while the works of modern deists are banned?

Why do we abandon to sneers and neglect that great mass of men who cultivate the earth that we may eat of its fruits, while we pay court to the useless men who live by their labor?

Why is there no place on earth where there are not more insects than men?

Why, since we are always complaining of our ills, are we always doing something to redouble them? Why, since we are so miserable, is it thought that to die is bad — when it is perfectly clear that not to have been alive, before birth, was not bad?

Why do we exist? In fact, why does anything exist?

RIGHT

AT THE time when France went wild over the system of Law, a man (who was always right) came to the controller-general who was then in office and said:

"Sir, you are completely mad. You think that we can increase the national wealth by printing paper money. This is not wealth, but only a sham for the real wealth of produce and manufacture. What you should have increased was our production of grain, wine and linen, making sure it found a market. But you make ten times as much in paper notes as we have actual wealth in money and goods; you are ten times mad."

No sooner had he finished than he was conducted to the lock-up of St. Lazarus. After a period during which he had plenty of time to improve his sense of the rightness of things, he was released. Thereupon he went straight to Rome and demanded a public audience so that he might not be interrupted. This is how he addressed the pope:

"Holy Father, you do everything contrariwise to the way Christ instructed. He was poor and you are very rich. He paid tribute and you exact it. He submitted to the powers that be and you have become one of them. He wandered on foot and you visit Castle Gandolfo in a splendid carriage. He ate whatever people gave him; you would have us eat fish on Fridays even though we reside far from rivers or the sea. I revere you, however, for everything else you do, so please give me an indulgence."

When he was at last released from the Castle St. Angelo he proceeded to Venice and asked an audience with the doge.

"Your serenity," he began, "don't you look pretty foolish, marrying the sea every year? In the first place, people have to marry the same person only once; in the second, your marriage is only half performed, like Harlequin's, because it lacks the consent of one of the parties; in the third, one of these days the other maritime powers will ridicule you for being unable to consummate the marriage."

After a stay under the leads of the doge's palace he was let out and proceeded to Constantinople, where he obtained an interview with the mufti and thus addressed him:

"Your religion has some good points, such as the worship of the Supreme Being, and the obligation of being just and charitable, but it is really nothing more than a hash of Judaism mixed with Mother Goose rhymes. If the archangel Gabriel had actually brought the leaves of the Koran to Mahomet, in all of Arabia someone would have seen him, whereas nobody did. Mahomet was therefore a big impostor, who deceived poor ignorant people." He had scarcely finished the last word before he was impaled.

Nevertheless he had been right all along.

SELF-LOVE

A BEGGAR in Madrid was asking alms; a passer-by said to him, "Aren't you ashamed to beg like this, when you can work?" "Sir," replied the mendicant, "I ask you for money, not advice," and he turned his back with true Castilian dignity. The beggar was haughty; his vanity was easily wounded; he asked alms out of self-love, and would not suffer reprimand out of even greater self-love.

A missionary in India saw a fakir loaded with chains, naked as an ape, lying on his belly and lashing himself for the sins of his fellows, who gave him coins. "What self-renouncement!" said a spectator. "Self-renouncement!" repeated the fakir scornfully, "I lash myself in this world only to serve you the same in the next, when you will be the horse and I the rider."

Whoever said that self-love is the basis of all our emotions and actions was right; it isn't necessary to prove that men have faces, nor that they possess self-love. It is the instrument of our preservation: it is like a provision for perpetuating mankind; it is essential, it is dear to us, it is delightful, and it should be hidden.

SLAVERY

WHEN I was at my country place at Mount Krapak I read a book full of wit and paradox in the manner of Montesquieu, against whom, as a matter of fact, it was written, which maintained that slavery is to be preferred to free labor. Pity those unhappy free men, it said, who must earn their livelihood when they can! No one has the responsibility of looking after them or feeding them, whereas slaves are fed and sheltered like horses. True enough; but human beings prefer to provide for themselves, and horses bred in freedom need no stables.

The book justly remarks that workmen lose many days when they cannot work — but this is not because they are independent, but because of ridiculous hindrances put between them and their production. It asserts, again with truth, that princes enfranchised their serfs through avarice. To get the money laboriously amassed by these unhappy souls they signed their letters of manumission. They did not bestow liberty, they sold it. Emperor Henry V began it by freeing the serfs of Spires and Worms in the twelfth century. The kings of France followed his example. Nothing tends more to prove the value of liberty than the high price these laboring men paid for it.

It is really for the man most affected to decide what state he prefers. Ask the humblest toiler, ragged, with only a crust of black bread, a bed of straw, and a hut half open to the elements, whether he would rather be a slave, better fed, clothed, and bedded. He will recoil with horror at the proposal.

TESTICLES

THE etymology of this word is obscure; it seems to mean *little witnesses*. Sixtus V, in his letter of 25 June 1587 to his nuncio in Spain, ordered him to unmarry all who were not possessed of testicles, by which order (executed by Philip II) it seems that there were many Spanish husbands lacking these organs.

A prejudice has long been entertained in the Russian Church that it is not lawful to say mass without testicles; at least they must be somewhere about the officiator, say in his pocket. This idea originated at the Council of Nice, which forbade admission into orders of any who were mutilated. The example of Origen, and of certain enthusiasts who had emasculated themselves, gave cause for the edict, which was reiterated at the Council of Arles.

The Greek Church did not bar from the altar those who had undergone the operation of Origen against their consent. The patriarchs of Constantinople: Nicetas, Ignatius, Photius, and Methodius were eunuchs. This point of discipline seems undecided, at the time of my writing, in the Catholic Church. It appears that a eunuch would require a dispensation to become ordained as a priest. Exclusion of eunuchs from the altar is paradoxical, as the service exacts chastity; such priests would certainly be tempted less in having to confess pretty girls.

UNDRESS

WHY do we hasten to lock up a man found undressed in the street, when we take no offense at statues in the same state, or paintings of Jesus and Mary Magdalen in certain churches? It is probable that man got along for a good while before he discovered raiment. In more than one South Sea island, and in America, there are still people ignorant of the art of the tailor.

The more civilized primitive peoples deck their privy parts with leaves, rushwork, and feathers. Is this the concealment of modesty or the veiling of what nature provokes our desire to discover?

There are saints of Islam who go about bare as apes. It is possible that such madmen think it more proper to present themselves before the Deity as He made them, than under disguises of their own invention. Or they may have exposed themselves in an ecstasy of chastity, for there are so few well-made specimens of either sex that nakedness does nothing to arouse desire.

In even more polished levels of culture there are sects which, in worshiping God, deprive themselves of clothing. Such have been the Adamites and the Abelians, who assembled naked to sing the praises of God. It is also recorded that the Abelians renounced marriage. If they had very many lusty youths or amorous maidens, they could not have been too much

like St. Adhelm or the happy Robert D'Ar-
briselle, who lay with the most luscious of ladies
only to prove the strength of their continence.

I must confess to thinking that it must have
been pleasant to see a hundred naked Helens
and Parises singing anthems, giving one another
the kiss of peace, and performing the ceremonies
of the *agapae*.

USAGES

NATIONS should not be judged by their usages
and popular superstitions. Had Caesar, in the
interest of promoting Roman commerce, sent
ambassadors to China, the emperor Yventi who
then reigned in China, and who is represented in
the annals as a wise and scholarly prince, after
receiving them with all Chinese politeness,
would have informed himself secretly of the
usages, sciences, and religion of the Romans.
His advisor would have told him that their
priests counted years in so absurd a manner that
the sun was already in the spring solstice when
the Romans were celebrating the first feasts of
winter; that a college of abracadabra was supported at great expense to tell just when to start
on a journey or fight a battle, which was found
by inspecting a bullock's liver or watching how
a chicken pecked its grain; and that, although
the people worshiped a supreme and only deity,
they also had many others — the good women
having little household gods, *penates*, four or

five inches high, including a goddess of bosoms and another of posteriors. But instead of laughing at all this, Yventi, being as just as he was polite, would have asked the ambassadors questions, and would have learned that Caesar had recently reformed the calendar, and that the college of augurs was a survival of barbarous times, which Caesar never consulted — in fact, Cicero, a great orator and philosopher, had written a book against it, called *Of Divination*. The emperor would have been given the book, read it with the aid of a translator, and been moved to admiration not only of the work but of the Roman republic.

VIRTUE

SUPPOSE that a hermit be gluttonous, drunken, and given over to self-debauch; he is vicious. Or say that if he have contrary qualities he is virtuous. I cannot agree to this. He is vile if he has the faults mentioned, but he is not vicious, wicked, or punishable by society, for his infamies do it no harm. It may be presumed that if he were to re-enter society he would not adorn it; he would indeed be wicked. And it is certain that the other hermit, the temperate and chaste one, would be a good man; for in society faults augment and good qualities diminish.

Nero, Pope Alexander VI, and other monsters of the kind have done good deeds. If they did, they were virtuous at the time. Certain theologians have said that the divine Marcus Aurelius was not virtuous, that he was a misled stoic who, not content with commanding men, would be esteemed by them besides; that he gave himself credit for the good which he did mankind; that all his life he was just, industrious, and beneficent through vanity; that he only deceived men by his virtues. To this I exclaim, O Lord, let us have more such sinners!

WAR

ALL animals are forever warring; each kind is born to devour another. Not even the gentle sheep and dove fail to take life in eating, if you consider the tiny organisms that inhabit a blade of grass or husk of seed. Males fight each other for females, like Menelaus and Paris. Air, land, and sea are theaters of unceasing combat.

God gave reason to man; using it, he should scorn to debase himself by aping animals, especially since he has neither natural equipment for killing nor instinct for sucking blood.

None will disagree that war brings pestilence and famine in its wake, after seeing the hospitals of the German army, or the villages in which some great exploit of war has taken place.

Peoples fall upon one another, not only without personal interest in the affair, but without knowing what it is all about. Five or six belligerent powers, three against three, two against four, or one against five, all detesting one another, unite and attack by turns; the only point of agreement is to do as much harm as possible.

The most wonderful part of the infernal business is that each leader of murderers causes his colors to be blessed and, before setting out on carnage, piously invokes God. If a leader kills only a couple of thousands he renders no thanks to God for so small a favor, but when he has wiped out ten thousand by fire and sword, and leveled a town to the ground, he bursts out into a paean of thanksgiving. Orators are paid to celebrate the slaughter, and to cite precedents from ancient Palestine. When there is no victory to eulogize, these orators fill in their time declaiming against vices: they show that women who put carmine on their cheeks will be consumed in red fire, that certain plays are works of the devil, and that folk who can pay ninety cents a pound for fresh fish during Lent will achieve their salvation, while others who can afford to eat only hamburger will go to perdition.

Miserable physicians of the soul, for an hour and a half you hold forth on pin-pricks, but utter never so much as a word about the malady which decimates us! Philosophers, moralists, burn your books! While the whim of a few men makes heroes of those who loyally murder, can you ply your trades?

What's the use of humanity, beneficence, modesty, temperance, mildness, wisdom, and piety if a couple of ounces of lead go through me and I die at the age of twenty in inexpressible torments, amidst a thousand of my dying comrades, while my eyes open for the last time on the sight of the town where I was born going up in flames, and my ears hear as their last sound the cries of women and children perishing under the ruins? And all for the interest of some man I do not even know!

WOMEN

WOMEN are usually less strong than men, smaller, and more apt to tire. Their flesh is less firm, their hair longer, their limbs rounder, their mouths smaller, their hips more prominent, and their bellies larger. These physical points distinguish women everywhere, from Lapland to Guinea, and from America to China.

Plutarch supposes that they are not so easily intoxicated with wine as men, because their composition is more liquid to begin with. They live somewhat longer than men; that is, you find more old women than old men. Those who seek causes say that nature gives them a longer life to recompense them for their trouble in bringing children into the world. But it is unlikely that nature bestows such compensation as this.

There are, of course, women with extraordinary strength and courage, who fight like men on equal terms and undergo prodigious labor; but these examples are rare. Leading a more sedentary life than men, women possess more gentleness of character, and are less prone to commit major crimes. This fact is undeniable; in all civilized countries fifty men at least are executed to every woman.

Mahomet limits the number of wives that a man may have to four. But as he has to be rich in order to support this many, few except great lords can avail themselves of this privilege. A plurality of wives has therefore done less harm in the Mahometan countries than we wish to suppose; it certainly does not produce the depopulation we read about.

Ben Abul Kiba, in his *Mirror of the Faithful*, relates that one of the viziers of the great Solyman addressed the following tirade to an envoy of Charles V: "Christian dog — for whom I have, however, a special esteem — do you reproach me with having four wives, according to our holy laws, while you empty a dozen barrels a year and I do not touch a single glass of wine?

What do you accomplish by passing more hours at table than I do in bed? I may get four children a year for the service of my august master, while you can scarcely produce one, so befuddled are you. And what would you have me do while a couple of my wives are far gone with child? What do you do during your wife's lyings-in?

"Suppose that in our wars against you Christian dogs we lose a hundred thousand soldiers. There we have, right off, a hundred thousand girls to provide for. Is it not for the wealthy to care for them? Evil betide any Mussulman so cold-hearted as not to take in four pretty girls as his legitimate wives, and to treat them as they merit! My conduct is restrained, considering Solomon's. What of the cock, the ram, the bull — has not every one of them his seraglio? Cease to accuse a sage of indulgence when he is content with so moderate a repast. I permit you to drink; allow me to love. You may change your wines; let me change my women."

"Dog of a Mussulman," replied the German, "for whom I have, however, a profound veneration, may I refute your arguments? If you have four wives you have four harpies, always backbiting, vexing, and fighting among themselves. Your house is a den of discord; none of them can love you, for each has only a quarter of you, and can bestow only a quarter of her heart in return. None of them can serve to make your life agreeable. They are prisoners. You are their absolute master and therefore they hate you. You are forced to guard them with eunuchs, who whip them when they are too happy. You compare yourself to a cock; a cock never has his pullets whipped by a capon. Pattern yourself as much as you want after animals; for my part, I want to love like a man. As for wine, it may be evil to drink in Arabia, but in Germany it is praiseworthy!"

ZEAL

IN RELIGION this is a pure and enlightened attachment to worship of the Divinity and its maintenance and progress; but when it grows blind and false and takes to persecution, it becomes the greatest scourge of humanity.

In government zeal is an enlightened attachment to the well-being of the governed, or at any rate it should be. But here too, when zeal